W9-BWD-991

WARS THAT CHANGED AMERICAN HISTORY

The Vietnam War

Michael Burgan

WORLD ALMANAC® LIBRARY

Please visit our Web site at: www.garethstevens.com
For a free color catalog describing World Almanac® Library's list of high-quality books
and multimedia programs, call 1-800-848-2928 (USA) or 1-800-387-3178 (Canada).
World Almanac® Library's fax: (414) 332-3567

Library of Congress Catalog-in-Publication Data

Burgan, Michael.
    The Vietnam War / by Michael Burgan. — North American ed.
        p. cm. — (Wars that changed American history)
    Includes bibliographical references and index.
    ISBN-10: 0-8368-7295-9 – ISBN-13: 978-0-8368-7295-8 (lib. bdg.)
    ISBN-10: 0-8368-7304-1 – ISBN-13: 978-0-8368-7304-7 (softcover)
    1. Vietnam War, 1961-1975—Juvenile literature.   2. Vietnam War, 1961-1975—United States—
Juvenile literature.   3. United States—Foreign relations—Vietnam—Juvenile literature.   4. Vietnam—
Foreign relations—United States—Juvenile literature.   I. Title.   II. Series.
    DS557.7.B893   2007
    959.704'3—dc22   2006011596

First published in 2007 by
World Almanac® Library
A Member of the WRC Media Family of Companies
330 West Olive Street, Suite 100
Milwaukee, WI 53212 USA

A Creative Media Applications, Inc. Production
Design and Production: Alan Barnett, Inc.
Editor: Susan Madoff
Copy Editor: Laurie Lieb
Proofreader: Laurie Lieb and Donna Drybread
Indexer: Nara Wood
World Almanac® Library editorial direction: Mark J. Sachner
World Almanac® Library editor: Alan Wachtel
World Almanac® Library art direction: Tammy West
World Almanac® Library production: Jessica Morris

Picture credits: The Bridgeman Art Library: page 5; Associated Press: pages 7, 8, 9, 11, 14, 16, 17,
20, 22, 23, 25, 26, 30, 31, 32, 34, 35, 37, 40, 42; Landov: page 13; The Getty Collection: page 29;
Maps courtesy of Ortelius Design

Printed in the United States of America

1 2 3 4 5 6 7 8 9 10 09 08 07 06

Table of Contents

Cover: U.S. paratroopers land and unload from a helicopter under heavy fire during the Vietnam War.

▼ Wars have shaped the history of the United States of America since the nation was founded in 1776. Conflict in this millennium continues to alter the decisions the government makes and the role the United States plays on the world stage.

From the time when America declared its independence in the 1700s to the present, every war in which Americans have fought has been a turning point in the nation's history. All of the major wars of American history have been bloody, and all of them have brought tragic loss of life. Some of them have been credited with great results, while others partly or entirely failed to achieve their goals. Some of them were widely supported; others were controversial and exposed deep divisions within the American people. None will ever be forgotten.

The American Revolution created a new type of nation based on the idea that the government should serve the people. As a result of the Mexican-American War, the young country expanded dramatically. Controversy over slavery in the new territory stoked the broader controversy between Northern and Southern states over the slavery issue and powers of state governments versus the federal government. When the slave states seceded, President Abraham Lincoln led the Union into a war against the Confederacy—the Civil War—that reunited a divided nation and ended slavery.

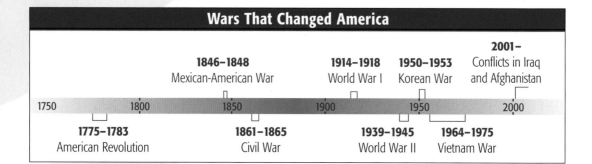

Wars That Changed America

	1846–1848 Mexican-American War		**1914–1918** World War I	**1950–1953** Korean War	**2001–** Conflicts in Iraq and Afghanistan
1750	1800	1850	1900	1950	2000
	1775–1783 American Revolution	**1861–1865** Civil War	**1939–1945** World War II	**1964–1975** Vietnam War	

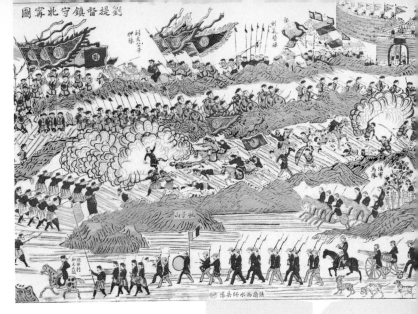

The roles that the United States played in World War I and World War II helped transform the country into a major world power. In both these wars, the entry of the United States helped turn the tide of the war.

Later in the twentieth century, the United States engaged in a Cold War rivalry with the Soviet Union. During this time, the United States fought two wars to prevent the spread of communism. The Korean War essentially ended in a stalemate, and after years of combat in the Vietnam War, the United States withdrew. Both claimed great numbers of American lives, and following its defeat in Vietnam, the United States became more cautious in its use of military force.

That trend changed when the United States led the war that drove invading Iraqi forces from Kuwait in 1990. After the al-Qaeda terrorist attacks of September 11, 2001, the United States again led a war, this time against Afghanistan, which was sheltering al-Qaeda. About two years later, the United States led the invasion that toppled Iraq's dictatorship.

In this book, readers will learn how the United States became involved in the Vietnam war and how U.S. involvement in the war escalated, reflecting the U.S. government's fear that the need to stop the spread of communism might lead the nation into a situation similar to its earlier participation in Korea. This ambivalence would mark the public's reaction to the war and ultimately cause the United States to officially pull its troops out after almost ten years of fighting, leading to the first loss in the nation's military history.

▲ A colored engraving from 1885 shows the Chinese defending the region of Bach Ninh during the Sino-French War. As a result of the war, France took control of lands including Vietnam, which they renamed French Indochina, that had been owned by China.

CHAPTER 1

Independence and Division

The roots of the long conflict in Vietnam sprang from the results of World War II. When World War II began, France controlled Vietnam, Laos, and Cambodia. Together, these three colonies were called French Indochina. The French had originally come to these lands to spread Roman Catholicism and compete with other European nations building empires in Asia. Over time, the French came to value Indochina's natural resources, such as rubber and tin.

In 1940, during World War II, Germany conquered France, and the next year Japan invaded Indochina. Japan left French officials in charge, since they knew the country and had experience running the government, but Japan held the true power in the country, thanks to its military strength in the region.

During World War II, U.S. president Franklin D. Roosevelt sometimes shifted his views on what should happen to Vietnam after the war, assuming that Japan would be defeated and therefore lose its control of Vietnam. After Roosevelt died in April 1945, the new president, Harry Truman, was faced with the problem.

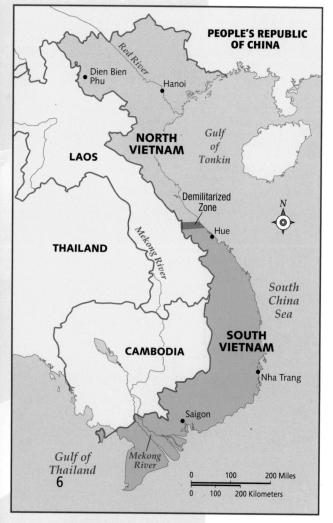

▼ A map of Vietnam in 1954 shows South Vietnam in green, North Vietnam in purple, and the demilitarized zone between the two nations in red.

PEOPLE'S REPUBLIC OF CHINA

Red River

Dien Bien Phu

Hanoi

NORTH VIETNAM

Gulf of Tonkin

LAOS

Demilitarized Zone

Hue

THAILAND

Mekong River

South China Sea

SOUTH VIETNAM

CAMBODIA

Nha Trang

Saigon

Gulf of Thailand

Mekong River

N

0   100   200 Miles

0   100   200 Kilometers

6

In July 1945, just before World War II ended, Truman met with leaders from Great Britain and the Soviet Union at the Potsdam Conference. Determined to ensure that Germany and Japan did not threaten world security again, these countries made plans to control the territories that had once been under German and Japanese influence. They agreed to let France resume control of Vietnam. World War II officially ended on September 2, when Japan signed a peace treaty with the United States and its **allies**. The United States was now the most powerful nation in the world, and it could influence the affairs of its allies, such as France. Even though France regained control in Vietnam, Truman and other U.S. officials hoped that France would one day grant Vietnam its independence. Meanwhile, a group of Vietnamese **nationalists** called the Vietminh had already gained control of part of Vietnam. Japan had lost its grip as it became clear it would lose the war. The same day the war ended, Ho Chi Minh, the leader of the Vietminh, declared Vietnam's independence. Ho called the new nation the Democratic Republic of Vietnam. Vietnam's emperor, Bao Dai, recognized the Vietminh as the new leaders. France, however,

▲ *French forces depart Indochina in 1955 under the terms of the Geneva Accords. At the close of World War II, the United States hoped that France would grant Vietnam independence, but its reluctance resulted in a victory for the Vietminh and a communist leader in control of part of the country.*

Fast Fact

Vietnam under French rule was actually made up of three smaller areas: Annam, Tonkin, and Cochin China.

Ho Chi Minh

Ho Chi Minh (1890–1969), pictured above, is considered the founder of the modern nation of Vietnam. As a young man, Ho worked as a sailor on French ships that often stopped at U.S. ports. Living for a time in France and also studying in the Soviet Union, Ho came to strongly favor independence for Vietnam. Ho also supported **communism** and opposed the political and economic systems used in the United States. During the 1930s, Ho founded Vietnam's first communist party and dedicated himself to winning Vietnam's independence from France. In Vietnam's wars against France (1946–1954) and then the United States (1964–1975), Ho willingly accepted help from the Soviet Union and other communist nations, although he wanted a Vietnam that was truly independent from any larger nation. His supporters called him "Uncle Ho," as "uncle" is a term of respect in Vietnam.

rejected Ho's claim of independence. Soon, French troops were battling the Vietminh for control of Vietnam.

Ho appealed to the United States for help against France. Truman, however, ignored Ho's appeal. The U.S. government disliked Ho's communist policies and thus favored restoring French rule in Indochina.

The French War

In 1946, fighting broke out between the French and the Vietminh in the northern port city of Haiphong. France soon controlled most of Vietnam's cities, including Saigon in the south and Hanoi in the north. The Vietminh dominated in the countryside. The peasants there had lived harsh lives of poverty under French rule, but since 1945, the Vietminh had stopped taxing the peasants and had given them land that used to belong to the French. In 1949, Bao Dai, who had previously worked with the Vietminh, agreed to work for France as the ruler of a country it called the State of Vietnam. France kept control of this new government, which was based in Saigon. Ho asserted that the Democratic Republic of Vietnam was the only legal government in the country.

Starting in 1950, the United States sent France money and supplies to battle the Vietminh. The United States viewed the Indochina War (the conflict between the French and Viet Minh forces for control of present-day Vietnam, Laos, and Cambodia) as part of a larger struggle called the **Cold War**. The United States saw the Soviet Union as a threat. Its leader, Joseph Stalin, a communist, talked about destroying **capitalism**, the economic system used in the United States. The communists also opposed the **democratic** governments that ruled in the United States and the other nations with democratic governments that banded together during World War II to fight against Germany, Italy, and Japan. Truman believed that the French were fighting the spread of communism in Asia by taking on Ho and the Vietminh. Dean Rusk, one of Truman's top advisers on foreign affairs, said that the Indochina War was "part of an international war" against communism.

In June 1950, communist forces from North Korea—with Soviet support—invaded South Korea. The United States led the effort to resist this invasion of South Korea, which was a U.S. ally. The war in Korea lasted until 1953. While fighting in Korea, the United States also increased its aid to France for the war in Vietnam. Altogether, the United States gave France $3 billion to fight the Vietminh. The United States also considered using some of its warplanes to aid France. President Dwight Eisenhower, however, decided that the United States should not get involved in another Asian war so soon after the end of the Korean War. He did not think he could convince U.S. allies to join the war, and he did not want the United States to fight it alone.

◀ French troops hold a communist Vietminh fighter at gunpoint on November 18, 1950. The captive stands with his hands over his head as one of the soldiers unfolds the Vietminh flag, which bears the communist symbol of a hammer and sickle.

The Chinese Revolution

Starting in the 1920s, Chinese communists began fighting a civil war in order to win control of the country. The United States supported the Chinese nationalists, who opposed communism. That aid, however, was not enough to defeat the communists, who took over China's government in 1949. The defeated nationalists then fled to the island of Formosa and formed their own nation, Taiwan. With the communist victory in China, U.S. leaders feared that the Chinese would try to spread communism throughout Southeast Asia. The Chinese did later aid Vietnamese communists in their war against the United States.

Fast Fact

Harry Truman's policy of stopping the spread of communism was called containment. As much as possible, he wanted to contain or limit communism to those countries where it already existed at the end of World War II.

Two Vietnams

In May 1954, the Vietnamese communists won a key battle at Dien Bien Phu, a village in northwestern Vietnam. After the French surrendered at Dien Bien Phu, several nations met in Geneva, Switzerland, to discuss the future of Indochina. These countries were France, Great Britain, the United States, the Soviet Union, and China. France and the Vietminh agreed to stop fighting. They also agreed that Vietnam would be an independent nation, split along the seventeenth parallel, a line of **latitude**. In the north, the Vietminh would rule, while Bao Dai would govern the south. Then, in 1956, residents in both halves of the country would vote for a new government to rule a reunited Vietnam. These agreements were known as the Geneva **Accords**.

Most of the other countries at the conference accepted this arrangement. The United States, however, did not sign any documents supporting this outcome, though it did not condemn the outcome either. U.S. leaders wanted the freedom to act in Vietnam in the future. They feared that the Vietminh would eventually rule all of Vietnam. John Foster Dulles was President Eisenhower's secretary of state—his top adviser in the **cabinet** for foreign affairs. Dulles said, "The United States should not stand...by and see the extension of communism by any means into Southeast Asia."

Ngo Dinh Diem was an official in the south who hated the Vietminh. U.S. officials chose to back him over Bao Dai as the leader of the new South Vietnam. Diem took power in 1955, and the United States began sending him money and weapons. Military advisers from the United States also arrived to train South Vietnamese troops.

In this way, the United States began to play a major role in an unsettled region.

The Vietnam War

CHAPTER 2

A Growing Presence

With U.S. support, Diem set up a new government in South Vietnam. He allowed only one political party—his own—and used its members to control the police and army. He also ignored the agreement made in Geneva in 1954 that Vietnam would hold national elections in 1956. Like U.S. leaders, Diem did not want a reunited Vietnam because he feared that the communists would take control. U.S. leaders supported Diem's refusal to hold the election, since they believed Ho would never allow a truly free vote in the north.

In the north, Ho also strengthened his power. He carried out land reform, which meant taking farms from wealthy landowners and giving them to peasant farmers. During this time, in 1955 and 1956, the Vietminh killed thousands of people who opposed the land reform and communist rule. Others who opposed Ho, including about one million Roman Catholics, fled to the south. Meanwhile, Ho had secretly left some Vietminh **cadres** in the south. Their mission was to pretend to be loyal to Diem—for a time. When they received word from North

▼ During a 1963 protest in Saigon, **Buddhist** monks and women attempt to pull down a barbed wire barricade erected to keep worshippers out of the Giac Minh Pagoda, a Buddhist temple built in 1744. The overwhelming majority of Vietnamese are Buddhists. Many Buddhists protested the government of Ngo Dinh Diem, the country's Catholic president, throughout the Vietnam War.

Vietnam, they would organize support for the Vietminh and seek to spread communism in the south.

The U.S. Role

During the first years after the 1954 Geneva Accords, the United States was secretly active in Vietnam. The Central Intelligence Agency (CIA) trained South Vietnamese soldiers and sent them to fight in the north. The leader of the CIA forces was Colonel Edward Lansdale. According to one CIA report from 1955, Lansdale's soldiers "had smuggled into Vietnam about 8.5 tons [7.7 metric tons] of supplies." The South Vietnamese failed in their missions in the north.The CIA had more success helping Diem fight groups in the south that opposed his rule.

From the start, the United States had mixed feelings about Diem. It favored his strong stance against communism, and between 1955 and 1959 President Eisenhower gave about $250 million each year to South Vietnam. But U.S. leaders saw that Diem was not winning the support of the average citizen in the south. His policies limited democracy and kept wealth and power mostly in the hands of his friends and family. Diem's actions made the average Vietnamese turn against his rule and become more willing to follow the communists. Adding to Diem's trouble were the communist cadres. At first, these Vietminh followed their orders to avoid violence. But as Diem's police arrested and killed more suspected communists, the cadres decided to fight back. By 1958, small groups of armed Vietminh and others who disliked Diem were roaming the countryside. Diem called them and others who opposed his rule the Vietcong, using a slang term for Vietnamese communists.

In 1959, North Vietnam decided to send aid to the Vietcong and actively fight Diem. The Vietcong carried out assassinations of local leaders loyal to Diem. The next year, Ho and his advisers created a new organization in the south, the National Liberation Front (NLF). It called for ending Diem's rule. Within the first year of its founding, the NLF had 300,000 members. The Vietcong served as its fighting force.

The increasing violence in South Vietnam alarmed the United States, which sent more military advisers, though by 1961 the total was still under one thousand. Early that year, Edward Lansdale sent a report to Washington that the Vietcong hoped to win in the south that year "and are much further along...than I had realized." If the south fell, Lansdale warned, "the remainder of Southeast Asia will be easy pickings for our enemy." Lansdale was describing what was sometimes called the domino theory. During the Cold War, the United States feared that if one nation came under communist control, it would be used as a base from which to spread communism throughout the region.

◀ *Female volunteers of a community defense organization patrol the village of Ben Cat, 31 miles (50 km) outside of Saigon, to discourage infiltration by Vietcong troops in January 1960.*

▲ Sergeant Stanley Harold of San Augustine, Texas, trains South Vietnamese soldiers in ambush techniques along the Laos border in August 1962. The soldiers' objective was to stop the flow of supplies traveling along the Ho Chi Minh Trail to communist Vietcong troops.

Kennedy and Vietnam

Lansdale wrote his report just as John F. Kennedy was preparing to become the new U.S. president. Kennedy was a strong anticommunist, and he favored increased aid to Diem. Kennedy secretly sent more advisers to Vietnam and allowed them to fight alongside the South Vietnamese army, called the Army of the Republic of Vietnam (ARVN). He also approved new raids in the north, using South Vietnamese **commandos** trained by the CIA. Americans, however, were not told that U.S. "advisers" were fighting the Vietcong. Kennedy wanted to continue the United States' public acceptance of the Geneva Accords. He did not want to admit that the United States was breaking the agreement that limited the number of foreign military personnel in Vietnam.

By the end of 1961, the United States had more than three thousand men in South Vietnam. They included advisers and a small number of specially trained troops. During the next year, the first U.S. helicopters arrived. They were useful for taking troops and supplies into remote areas. Slowly, the number of U.S. casualties began to grow, as more troops became actively involved in the fighting. Now, the press was openly reporting on the increased activity by U.S. "advisers."

At this time, the NLF and the Vietcong were also increasing their forces. Diem had not changed his methods, and more Vietnamese were ready to join the Vietcong and fight to get rid of him. To try to weaken the Vietcong, the United States and South Vietnam began a new policy. They moved peasants off their farms into heavily guarded villages, called strategic hamlets. Diem and U.S. leaders hoped the move would protect the peasants from attack and also make it harder for them to give aid to the Vietcong. Some farmers disliked being forced from their homes, and they turned against Diem and his rule. Many of these new towns were also not well defended. The strategic hamlet policy quickly ended.

In 1963, Diem made even more enemies in the south by clamping down on Buddhists. As a Roman Catholic, he disliked their religion, and he feared that many Buddhists were not loyal to his government. Under Diem's orders, Buddhists were not allowed to fly their flag in public. Then, soldiers fired on Buddhists who had gathered to protest Diem's policies against them. One of the Buddhist leaders met with U.S. officials in Saigon, the capital of South Vietnam. He told the Americans, "You are responsible for the present trouble because you back Diem and his government of ignoramuses." By the fall of 1963, Kennedy realized he did have a problem with Diem. Kennedy decided to support a coup d'état—a sudden takeover of the government—designed to replace Diem with a new government.

On November 1, a group of South Vietnamese generals took control of the government. Henry Cabot Lodge, the top U.S. **diplomat** in Saigon, had told the generals that the United States would not stop the coup. They arrested Diem and his brother. Later, the two men were killed. After the coup, Lodge told the generals, "The prospects now are for a shorter war." Kennedy must have hoped that was true, but he would not see how the war turned out. On November 22, 1963, he was assassinated in Dallas, Texas. Vice President Lyndon B. Johnson became president. He would make the next major decisions about the U.S. role in Vietnam.

John Paul Vann

One of the best known of the U.S. advisers was Lieutenant Colonel John Paul Vann. He was featured in two books about the early years of the war. Vann thought the South Vietnamese could win "if someone shows them how." He also spoke openly, however, when things went bad, such as when a heavily outnumbered Vietcong force defeated ARVN troops and killed several U.S. soldiers at Ap Bac early in 1963. Vann's willingness to talk to reporters gave Americans a different view of the war compared to what most U.S. officials said. Other military leaders tried to ignore Vann because they wanted to believe—and convince Americans—that the war was going better than it was. Vann died in Vietnam in 1965.

Fast Fact

In July 1959, the Vietcong attacked an air base in South Vietnam. Two U.S. soldiers stationed there were killed. They are often considered the first official American **casualties** of the Vietnam War.

CHAPTER 3

A Real War

▼ *General Maxwell Taylor, President Kennedy's special military adviser in Vietnam, inspects a cannon on the front line along the South Vietnam–North Vietnam border in October 1961.*

As vice president, Lyndon Johnson had visited Vietnam and other countries in the region. After a 1961 trip he wrote, "The battle against communism in Southeast Asia must be joined with strength and determination." Johnson believed in the domino theory. And like other U.S. officials, he believed the North Vietnamese were carrying out orders from the Soviet Union and China. The United States thought that the Soviet Union and China worked together to help Ho. In reality, the two communist countries were competing for influence in North Vietnam. Ho was willing to accept help from either country, but he was determined to keep North Vietnam as independent as possible. Throughout the war, U.S. leaders did not realize how much Ho tried to act on his own. They always saw the Vietnam War as a part of the larger Cold War and not as Ho saw it—as a war for independence. The drive for independence made Ho and his supporters determined to win at any cost.

Soon after becoming president, Johnson met with his advisers. He told them he was "not going to lose Vietnam." Johnson wanted to convince the Soviets that he was tough and would fight to stop the spread of communism. Johnson also hoped that military success would win support in the United States for his **domestic** policies. He wanted to expand aid programs to the poor and protect the **civil rights** of African Americans.

Secret Battles

Early in 1964, President Johnson approved new **covert** operations against North Vietnam, hoping to cut off supplies from the north to the Vietcong. South Vietnamese commandos continued the attacks in the north begun under President Kennedy, blowing up bridges and railways. And in Laos, highly trained U.S. Army soldiers called Green Berets continued their secret mission of recruiting local residents to fight the communists.

In South Vietnam, U.S. pilots were now carrying out more missions against the Vietcong. In addition to helicopters, they now flew planes. At times, the planes were used to drop defoliants, chemicals that stripped the leaves off plants and trees. The bare trees made it harder for the Vietcong to hide from the ARVN. The planes also dropped bombs filled with napalm, a jelly-like material that starts fires when it hits a target. The napalm was used both to destroy forests and kill enemy troops.

In August 1964, the South Vietnamese carried out commando raids from small warships in the Gulf of Tonkin. Nearby were two U.S. naval ships, the *Maddox* and the *C. Turner Joy*. They were gathering **intelligence** by listening to North Vietnamese radio signals. On August 2, the *Maddox* came under attack from several small North Vietnamese boats. U.S. airplanes drove off the enemy ships. Two days later, both U.S. ships reported that they were under attack again.

Lyndon B. Johnson

Born on August 27, 1908, near Stonewall, Texas, Lyndon Baines Johnson, pictured above, entered politics during the 1930s. He served in the U.S. House of Representatives, then moved to the Senate in 1948. During most of the 1950s, he was the majority leader, the top position in the Senate. Johnson was famous for getting senators with opposing views to find agreement on important issues, such as civil rights. In 1960, Johnson hoped that his party, the Democrats, would choose him as its **candidate** for president. The Democrats chose John F. Kennedy instead, and he then chose Johnson as the vice presidential candidate. As president, Johnson's decisions to put large numbers of troops into Vietnam eventually made him unpopular, and he did not seek reelection in 1968. He retired to Texas, where he died in 1973.

For many years, some historians claimed that the second attack in the Gulf of Tonkin never took place. In 2005, the National Security Agency (NSA) released information that showed the truth of this claim. This government agency collects intelligence by listening to electronic messages, and in 1964, it knew that the North Vietnamese did not attack on August 4. Errors and a refusal to accept all the facts gathered led officials at the NSA to keep the truth from President Johnson and his advisers. Even at the time, however, some members of the U.S. government had doubts about the attack. Still, Johnson used this supposed attack as a reason for seeking the Gulf of Tonkin Resolution.

Fast Fact

The first U.S. bombing of North Vietnam was called Operation Rolling Thunder. It lasted for three years, during which U.S. planes dropped more than 640,000 tons (580,480 metric tons) of bombs.

Planes, however, did not see any sign of the enemy. Still, Johnson told Americans that there had been a second attack. Based on what was later called the Gulf of Tonkin incident, Congress passed a joint resolution giving Johnson the power to "take all necessary measures to repel any armed attack against the forces of the United States and to prevent further aggression." The Gulf of Tonkin Resolution meant that Johnson could increase U.S. involvement in Vietnam without a formal declaration of war approved by Congress.

Bombs and Soldiers

In response to the Gulf of Tonkin incident, U.S. warplanes bombed North Vietnamese naval bases. In the south, the Vietcong continued to receive aid from North Vietnam along the Ho Chi Minh Trail. Johnson ordered secret bombing of the trail and communist bases in Laos. Then, early in 1965, he announced a new plan to bomb North Vietnam itself. By this time, soldiers from the North Vietnamese Army (NVA) were helping the Vietcong fight in the south. Johnson wanted Ho to see that the United States opposed this new role that North Vietnam was playing in the war.

When the bombing began, Johnson had just entered his first full term as president. Within his cabinet, Johnson's advisers disagreed about what to do in Southeast Asia. Some called for vastly expanding the U.S. military presence. They were called "hawks," and they included Secretary of Defense Robert McNamara and National Security Adviser McGeorge Bundy. The advisers who did not want to increase the U.S. military presence were called "doves." George Ball, from the State Department, was the most vocal dove. As the war went on, hawks and doves debated how to carry on the war, and across the United States, the terms *hawk* and *dove* were commonly used.

The Vietnam War

Johnson had been elected in November 1964 after promising that he would not send "American boys nine or ten thousand miles [14,400 or 16,000 kilometers] away from home" to defend South Vietnam. In March 1965, however, Johnson ordered the first U.S. ground forces into the country. Several thousand U.S. Marines landed at Da Nang. Within a few months, the United States had eighty thousand troops in South Vietnam, under the command of General William Westmoreland. The general had convinced Johnson that only a larger U.S. military role would defeat the communists.

In November 1965, U.S. forces fought their first major battle against NVA troops at Ia Drang. Helicopters and bombers helped the Americans and ARVN drive off the enemy soldiers, after killing almost two thousand of them, but the Americans lost more than three hundred men of their own. The United States, it seemed, might defeat the North Vietnamese, but at a high cost.

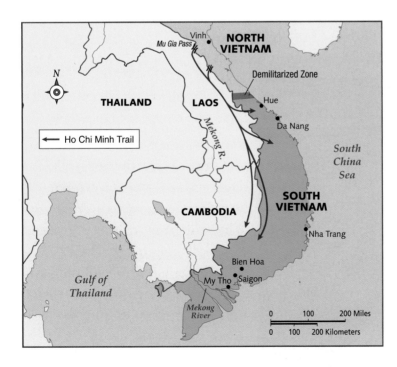

◀ A map of the Ho Chi Minh Trail (in purple) shows the jungle paths linking communist North Vietnam to regions outside of Saigon in South Vietnam. The trail, which ran through parts of Laos and Cambodia, consisted of pathways for foot and bicycle traffic and roads where trucks could travel. When the war started, the journey between the two end points of the trail took nearly six months on foot, but by the end of the war, because of heavy usage by both sides, the trip took only six weeks.

CHAPTER 4

The Home Front

As 1965 came to an end, the United States had 184,000 military personnel in Vietnam. President Johnson prepared to send even more troops overseas, and many young American men volunteered for the war. They thought it was their duty to fight communists. But part of the population started to question why the United States was fighting in Southeast Asia. These people began what became the largest antiwar movement in U.S. history. The first large protests against the Vietnam War occurred a month after U.S. ground troops landed at Da Nang. Thousands of protesters gathered in Washington, D.C., and at rallies at various colleges.

Some of the early protests were against the draft. During the years of the Vietnam War, more than eight million U.S. men volunteered for military service. More than two million, however, were taken into the military through the draft. Some draftees, like Dick Ellis of North Carolina, were proud to serve in Vietnam. The army tried to use any special skills the draftees had. When it could not use Ellis's talents as a TV weatherman, Ellis told his officers, "I'll be the best truck driver you've got."

▼ At a gathering of draft protesters outside the Federal Building in San Francisco, California, in October 1979, hands reach upward to drop draft cards into a basket to be presented to the U.S. district attorney, Cecil Poole.

Other draftees, however, opposed the war. Many protesters thought it unfair that young men who did not support the war should have to risk their lives fighting it. Some draftees refused to report for military service. Their refusal to serve was against the law, and some fled to Canada to avoid arrest.

Some American opponents of the war thought that even if the communists won in Vietnam, U.S. security was not at risk. Other protesters were drawn to the antiwar movement because they had been involved in the civil rights protests of the early 1960s. The civil rights movement called for justice and equality for African Americans. The war, some people thought, was taking attention and money away from the effort to ensure equality at home. African American soldiers were said to be defending democracy, yet many faced **discrimination** every day. Martin Luther King, Jr., a key leader of the civil rights movement, spoke out strongly against the war.

At times, U.S. soldiers themselves spoke out against the war. In 1966, one soldier wrote to his church in New York, describing how he "was sitting there in a uniform I detest, in a country that is involved in a war that I don't support." Some soldiers, after returning to the United States, formed an antiwar organization called Vietnam Veterans Against the War. Other U.S. troops, however, supported the war and disliked the protesters. They thought the protesters did not understand what was at stake in the war against communism—that the United States was fighting an enemy that wanted to destroy the American system of government.

The American "Counterculture"

Most of the young people serving in the military or protesting the Vietnam War were baby boomers,

The Changing Draft System

The draft system required all men over eighteen to register with the government. A certain number were picked at random to join the military. The draft system had been in place since 1940 to make sure that the military always had enough troops. The number of men drafted increased during wartime. At the start of the Vietnam War, the U.S. government took the oldest draftees first. Draftees could be excused, however, for poor health or other reasons. In 1969, the government changed to a lottery system, which made the draft more random. Young men born between 1944 and 1950 whose birthday was selected out of a bin containing a card for each day of the year had to report for military duty. The lottery sparked huge interest across the country, and television cameras recorded the selection of the first date— September 14.

▼ Folk singer Joan Baez (with guitar) sits on a street corner in San Francisco, performing for passersby. Baez, a familiar voice in the antiwar movement, wrote many songs protesting the Vietnam War.

born after World War II, when the United States saw a boom in population growth. Because of their large numbers, the boomers influenced U.S. culture. Seeing a large, young market, film and music companies sold products that appealed to young people, and ads suggested that being young was a good thing.

As the Vietnam War **escalated**, the antiwar movement blended with other movements and ideas promoted by many young Americans. Some believed that taking illegal drugs was a way to learn new things about themselves and the world. Others enjoyed loud rock music that seemed shocking to their parents. Young men began growing their hair long and people of both sexes wore wild clothes. Many of these young people, known as hippies, also opposed following rules set down by parents, teachers, and political leaders. The hippies opposed the war and talked about spreading peace and love around the world. People with these ideas became known as "the counterculture"—they were counter, or against, the main U.S. culture of the time. The antiwar protests became part of the counterculture as well.

Most American adults did not accept the values of the counterculture. They believed what Johnson and others said about the dangers of communism. They also believed in the importance of obeying the law. Antiwar protests seemed to threaten law and order, especially when students took over college buildings or clashed with police, as happened at the University of Wisconsin at Madison in 1967.

Riots that broke out in some cities also upset many Americans. In 1965, young African Americans rioted in Watts, a neighborhood in Los Angeles, California. Some were angry at the way local police treated them. Others were tired of living in poverty. The arrest of several people after a traffic stop eventually led to the Watts riot. Over the next two years, more riots followed in other cities. Some African American leaders, such as Martin Luther King, Jr., thought that U.S. leaders should be spending more time and money to help blacks achieve equal rights and better living conditions and that the money spent fighting the war in Vietnam could be put to better use at home. To some white Americans, the riots were frightening. The country seemed to be facing as great a threat from violence and disorder at home as it did overseas.

By 1967, almost 400,000 military personnel were in Vietnam, and more than 6,000 Americans had been killed since the war began. Protests grew larger, with 50,000 people attending one rally in Washington, D.C. At one point, police fired tear gas to drive away the protesters. One person there later recalled, "People became frightened. They began running every which way.... A sense of chaos took over." Through 1967, Johnson made fewer public speeches than usual in order to avoid being questioned about the war. That August, *Time* magazine wrote that he often worked in a small office in the White House, "strangely [cut off] from his countrymen's doubts and fears."

A Televised War

In August 1965, only 25 percent of the Americans who responded to a poll thought that the United States should not be fighting in Vietnam. Just over two years later, the number had almost doubled. The antiwar protests played a role in shaping this change in opinion. Even more important may have been the role of television. In Vietnam, for the first time ever, television cameras followed troops into battle. One early report was shown in August 1965 on the CBS network. The

Martin Luther King Jr.

Born in Atlanta in 1929, the Reverend Martin Luther King, Jr., pictured above, believed that African Americans could win equal rights without using violence. He became prominent in the civil rights movement in 1955, leading many protests throughout the south. As the Vietnam War grew, he turned his attention to the killing there. He said in 1967 that he had to speak out against "the greatest [source] of violence in the world today—my own government." Massive amounts of violence in Vietnam, King believed, would not make the United States safer. "Somehow this madness must cease," he said. King continued to work against the war and for civil rights until his assassination on April 4, 1968, in Memphis, Tennessee.

Music from a War

Music was an important part of the counterculture of the 1960s. Some folk and rock musicians wrote songs protesting the war. One talented songwriter, Bob Dylan, wrote antiwar songs such as "Masters of War." Groups such as Jefferson Airplane, Country Joe and the Fish, and the Doors also wrote songs that touched on the war and the general anger many young Americans felt toward the leaders of their country. One song that supported the war and U.S. troops was "The Ballad of the Green Berets," by Barry Sadler. The song referred to the troops as "America's best."

Fast Fact

From 1955 to 1975, sixty-three journalists were killed during fighting in Vietnam.

camera showed U.S. soldiers burning down the homes of Vietnamese **civilians**. The reporter noted that "a Marine platoon…wounded three women and killed one child." Images like these made many Americans question the country's purpose in Vietnam. Vietnamese women and children did not seem like a threat to the United States, although U.S. soldiers knew that many civilians helped the Vietcong or were communists themselves. Yet in the United States, more people started to believe that the harsh treatment of civilians and other **atrocities** were wrong. The daily news reports also reminded Americans of the growing number of U.S. troops killed and wounded.

General Westmoreland did not like having TV crews and reporters in the field. The U.S. government tried to shape what the media reported by giving reporters its version of events. Military officials held daily meetings with reporters in Saigon at 5 P.M. Reporters began calling these meetings the "five o'clock Follies." They seemed more of a show than an effort to tell the truth. Still, one reporter said that the Follies, "for all their failings, were not the pack of lies that some critics suggested." The best reporters balanced government views of the war with what they saw and heard themselves.

Some journalists openly opposed the war. Others changed their views as they reported on events in Vietnam. Neil Sheehan, of the *New York Times*, said in 1966 that he was "not a dove, but no longer a hawk." Two years later, Walter Cronkite said that the United States most likely could not win the war. Cronkite was the most popular TV newscaster in the country. President Johnson knew that many Americans respected Cronkite's views. After his comments, U.S. officials knew it would be hard to rebuild support for the war.

The Vietnam War

CHAPTER 5

Fighting the War

When deciding what to do about Vietnam, President Johnson had two main concerns. As he told the nation in April 1965, he wanted to preserve "the independence of South Vietnam, and its freedom from attack." But he did not want the war to take attention and money away from his Great Society domestic programs. Johnson and his advisers wanted to fight what they called a limited war. The United States would attack North Vietnam by air to weaken its ability to arm its troops and the Vietcong. In the south, U.S. troops would try to stop the Vietcong from controlling territory. Over time, the Americans hoped, the communists would see they could not take over South Vietnam and would stop fighting. Johnson also hoped that the war would end before many more U.S. troops died in battle.

▼ A U.S. B-52 Stratofortress—a long-range, heavy bomber plane—drops a load of 750-pound (341-kilogram) bombs over the North Vietnam coast in November 1965.

Guns and Butter

President Johnson resisted Robert McNamara's call for a special war tax to pay for the Vietnam War. His decision to spend heavily on both guns and "butter"—Great Society programs—helped the U.S. economy grow during the mid-1960s. But this decision also led to a large deficit, meaning that the country spent more money than it took in.

▼ In June 1965, U.S. soldiers search for Vietcong hideouts in the swampy jungle in Chutes de Trian, 40 miles (64 km) northeast of Saigon.

The U.S. plan was limited because it did not involve attacking North Vietnam with ground troops. U.S. leaders feared that a military invasion of the north would lead the Soviet Union or China to take direct action against the United States. Such an escalation of the war raised the risk of one side or the other using nuclear weapons. Nuclear weapons release a powerful form of energy called radiation. The explosive force of these weapons and their radiation could have killed tens of thousands of people in an instant. One military official was heard to say, "It might be a good idea to toss in a nuke from time to time, just to keep the other side guessing." But McNamara said, "There was no way...President Johnson would have authorized their use." Johnson told another aide he feared that any direct fighting with the Soviets would mean that "I've got World War III on my hands."

In the Field

The Vietnam War was not like other wars Americans had fought. During World War II and the Korean War, large numbers of enemy forces met in battle, with each side firing **artillery**. The Vietcong and NVA, however, often used guerrilla tactics. This meant that small groups of soldiers attacked enemy camps, then ran off before the Americans or South Vietnamese could respond. The communist troops often dressed as civilians, making it hard for their opponents to know who was a friend and who was a foe.

Adding to the U.S. soldiers' difficulties were the land and climate in Vietnam. The country was filled with hills and thick jungles where the enemy could easily hide. The weather was often hot and rainy, and soldiers had trouble keeping themselves and their equipment dry. Philip Caputo served in Vietnam in 1965 and later wrote about his experiences. He said, "It would rain 24 hours a day for a week, two weeks, sometimes three at a time. You were constantly drenched." Another problem was illness: many U.S. soldiers battled diseases linked to the tropical climate, such as malaria and various skin disorders.

To fight the guerrillas, General Westmoreland used a tactic called "search and destroy." Most U.S. forces stayed at bases near Saigon or along the coast. The bases were easier to defend than camps set up in the jungles. From the bases, teams of soldiers searched for the guerrillas' bases and then destroyed them. The plan, however, was not always effective. The Vietcong could usually slip out of a camp or village before the U.S. attack. After the Americans left, the guerrillas would return. The U.S. attacks destroyed some villages, causing the civilian residents to hate the American troops and become even more likely to support the Vietcong.

Along with the ground fighting, the U.S. Air Force continued to bomb targets in North Vietnam. U.S. planes also attacked the Ho Chi Minh Trail. The U.S. Navy played a part as well. Navy planes were launched from aircraft carriers, small boats patrolled the rivers and coasts of Vietnam, and larger ships sometimes fired their guns at communist targets on shore. Although called a limited war, the fighting in Vietnam involved all branches of the U.S. military.

Some of the action continued to be covert. Johnson would not let U.S. troops go into North

Eyewitness to the Fighting

Ward Just, a reporter traveling with U.S. troops, described the fighting on a U.S. mission:

The fighting came from three sides, hitting the Americans at all points on the trail.... Only a few actually saw the enemy, who were [moving] and firing as they [moved].... The reports were only that there were a lot of enemy, and it was impossible to tell how many.... They had grenades and small arms and automatic weapons, and good cover to shoot from. They fought from concealed positions and they had the element of surprise and knowledge of the [land]. It was, after all, their base camp.

Fast Fact

The largest U.S. bomber used during the Vietnam War was the B-52. It could carry up to 35 tons (32 metric tons) of bombs and fly for more than 8,000 miles (12,872 km) without stopping.

Women at War

American women played a part in the Vietnam War. At the time women in the military were not allowed to serve in any combat roles (today women hold a small number of combat positions). Still, about seventy-five hundred women went to Vietnam as part of the military. Most served as nurses or held office jobs. Eight women serving in the U.S. armed forces were killed during the Vietnam War, as well as fifty-nine female American civilians.

Vietnam and Laos, which General Westmoreland later called "a major problem" since the communists could flee to those countries to avoid U.S. troops. Small groups of U.S. Special Forces, however, did operate beyond the borders of South Vietnam. These soldiers used weapons and clothes that came from other countries, so, if they were killed, their supplies could not be traced back to the U.S. military. By this time, the Ho Chi Minh Trail was more than a jungle path. The communists had turned it into a major road, used by trucks, carts, and soldiers on foot. The Special Forces placed sensors along the trail to pick up sounds. The sensors helped the Americans know when the trail was being used, so they could carry out air strikes against it.

Changes for the Worse

By the end of 1967, almost 500,000 U.S. troops were in Vietnam. About 10,000 were killed that year, and another 62,000 were wounded. General Westmoreland thought that the United States was killing an even larger number of enemy troops. By this time, more of the fighting was being done by the NVA, not guerrillas from the south. The United States was also practicing a tactic called "clear and hold." U.S. troops cleared out enemy soldiers from a village or region, and then South Vietnamese troops remained to prevent the communists from returning. The Americans and their allies wanted to win the support of South Vietnamese civilians by convincing them that they would be protected from communist attacks. The South Vietnamese government was **corrupt**, however, and few peasants trusted their leaders to protect their lives or work for their interests. The United States hoped to build that trust, but at times American soldiers still killed civilians, weakening those efforts.

One of the turning points of the war came on January 30, 1968. The day was Tet, the Vietnamese New Year. A few small communist attacks that day turned into a major **offensive** against U.S. troops stationed in Saigon and other cities in the south. Some of the worst fighting took place in and around the city of Hue. The communists committed atrocities against civilians there, and the U.S. forces battled for several weeks before retaking the city. In the end, the Tet offensive was a military failure for the communists. They could not hold the cities they attacked and they did not win the popular support from South Vietnamese civilians they had hoped for. But in some ways, the loss was also a victory. The North Vietnamese had successfully brought men and supplies into the south, even though so many U.S. soldiers were stationed there. They also killed several thousand U.S. and ARVN troops. Finally, in the United States, the Tet offensive upset many Americans. They read about Vietcong troops inside the U.S. **Embassy** in Saigon. They saw a picture of a South Vietnamese general executing a captured enemy soldier, the general's gun just inches from the man's head. Many Americans began to wonder if the war was going as well as Johnson often said it was.

After the Tet offensive, several things changed. General Westmoreland wanted another 200,000 troops, but Johnson decided to end the escalation of the war. He agreed to send only an additional 13,500. The president also decided to limit bombing in the north and called for direct peace talks with the communists. "There is no need," he said, "to delay the talks that could bring an end to this long and bloody war." Johnson then announced that he would not run for president again that November.

My Lai

In March 1968, U.S. troops led by Lieutenant William Calley killed about five hundred unarmed civilians at the village of My Lai. The attack was later called the My Lai massacre, and it was the worst atrocity committed by U.S. troops during the Vietnam War. The U.S. military did not admit that the massacre had taken place until one year later, when it was reported in the media. Calley was sent to prison for his role in the incident, which led many Americans to question how the war was being fought.

CHAPTER 6

Nixon's Plans

▼ Presidential candidate Richard Nixon greets the crowd on a campaign visit to Springfield, Missouri, in September 1968.

In January 1969, Richard Nixon, a Republican, was sworn in as president of the United States. By this time, Johnson had halted the bombing of North Vietnam, and U.S. officials were holding peace talks with the North and South Vietnamese. The talks, however, had stalled. Nixon hoped he could use diplomacy to end the war, yet at the same time he wanted the communists to think he would still take military action when necessary. He even hinted that he might use nuclear weapons, risking a nuclear attack by China or the Soviet Union in return. Nixon did not really plan to use those weapons, but he wanted North Vietnam to believe he might. To one aide, he called this "the madman theory."

New Policies for the War

To help him shape his policy on the war, Nixon chose Henry Kissinger as his national security adviser. His secretary of defense was Melvin Laird. General Creighton Abrams had just replaced Westmoreland as the commander of U.S. troops in Vietnam. In February, Nixon decided to launch secret bombing raids on NVA troops based in Cambodia. Nixon hoped the attacks would convince the

North Vietnamese to take the peace talks seriously. Doing "something on the military front," he said, was "something they will understand." Some newspapers reported that U.S. planes attacked Cambodia, but Nixon did not publicly reveal the details of the size of the mission until months later.

At the same time, Nixon wanted to let the ARVN do more of the fighting in South Vietnam. The United States would give the ARVN better weapons and more training, and its increased role would let Nixon pull out some U.S. troops. Laird called this process the "Vietnamization" of the war. Under this new policy, fewer young Americans were drafted, and U.S. soldiers stationed in Vietnam began to return to the United States.

In July, Nixon wrote directly to Ho Chi Minh, calling for serious peace talks. Nixon had already said that the U.S. troops would leave Southeast Asia if the NVA pulled out of South Vietnam. In August, Ho responded. He told Nixon that the Vietnamese were "determined to fight to the end…in order to defend their country and their sacred national rights." A week later, Ho died, but the other North Vietnamese communist leaders were equally dedicated to winning the war. At the same time, Nixon had Kissinger secretly contact the Soviet Union and China. Nixon hoped to improve relations with those powerful communist nations, which then might be willing to influence North Vietnam to talk seriously about peace.

While these efforts went on, many Americans continued to protest the war. In the fall of 1969, hundreds of thousands of protesters gathered in New York, Washington, and other cities. By this time, not everyone who opposed the war was a hippie or college student. Many professors at major universities opposed the war, and members of Congress and

Henry Kissinger

Henry Kissinger, pictured above, was born in Germany and came to the United States as a boy in 1933. He served in World War II, then later became a professor of foreign policy. His specialty was nuclear weapons—if and when they should be used during wartime. In 1967, during the presidential campaign, Kissinger questioned Nixon's ability to end the war—he called Nixon "the most dangerous, of all the men running, to have as president." But in November 1968, he agreed to become Nixon's national security adviser and later also served as secretary of state. Kissinger shared the 1973 Nobel Peace Prize for his efforts to end the Vietnam War. He also won praise for trying to improve U.S. relations with China and the Soviet Union. Critics noted, however, that he backed some of the major escalations of the war under Nixon, including the secret bombing of Cambodia and attacks on Laos.

▼ A U.S. Special Forces officer yells to his troops to move forward toward a hilltop outpost in Ha Thanh, 325 miles (523 km) northeast of Saigon. In September 1968, the outpost was overrun by North Vietnamese troops as the U.S. Army was attempting to reclaim the region.

current and former members of the military were also speaking out against it.

New Battles, New Peace Talks

On the battlefield, Vietnamization seemed to have some success. With better training and weapons, the ARVN did well against the Vietcong. But most South Vietnamese citizens still did not support their government. In the years since the assassination of Ngo Dinh Diem, the country's leaders had remained corrupt. Since 1967, former general Nguyen Van Thieu had been in charge.

In 1970, the main military action of the United States was in Laos and Cambodia. U.S. planes continued to bomb the Ho Chi Minh Trail and attacked bases used by the NVA and Vietcong. On the ground, the ARVN and Cambodian anticommunists battled communist forces. On April 30, Nixon announced that U.S. ground troops would enter Cambodia for a limited time to help fight the NVA there. Soon, new protests broke out on college campuses. Nixon, however, kept his word and did not keep the U.S. ground forces in Cambodia. Still, U.S. planes continued to bomb in that country.

By the start of 1971, the number of U.S. troops in Vietnam had fallen to 334,600, but the total number killed had risen to more than 44,000. Lieutenant William Calley had been found guilty for his role in the My Lai massacre, and news of his military trial focused attention on U.S. atrocities.

Nixon also faced another problem connected to the war. The *New York Times* began publishing a secret history of the U.S. role in Vietnam. Robert McNamara, the former secretary of defense, had ordered the history written in 1968. Now, Americans learned that at times their presidents had lied about U.S. activities in Vietnam. Although the history, known as the *Pentagon Papers*, did not deal with Nixon's presidency, he was angry about its publication. Some of the information revealed how the United States collected intelligence. Nixon worried that because Americans now knew they had been lied to before, they might doubt what he told them about the war and would be less likely to support his plans. Nixon created a secret White House team called "the plumbers" whose job was to keep secrets about the war and other government activities from reaching the media.

In 1972, the North Vietnamese began a major offensive in the south. U.S. troop strength had fallen to 160,000, and many of the soldiers who remained had low spirits. Some refused orders to fight. A tiny number took the extreme step of killing their own officers. The ARVN also suffered from low morale at times. In April, one U.S. officer told a reporter, "Things are getting worse and worse and the Vietnamese just aren't doing anything." By this time, huge areas of Vietnam had been destroyed by more than a decade of war.

While the fighting continued, Henry Kissinger held secret talks with the North Vietnamese. By this time, Nixon had made news by becoming the first U.S. president to visit the Soviet Union and China. The leaders of those two communist countries told North Vietnam to consider ending the war. Meanwhile, heavy U.S. bombing in the north also made the North Vietnamese seriously consider peace. Near the end of 1972, the two sides seemed to have reached a peace agreement. The U.S. military role in Vietnam was almost over.

The Kent State Shootings

On May 4, 1970, members of the Ohio National Guard killed four students at Kent State University during an antiwar protest in response to President Nixon's sending U.S. troops into Cambodia. Governor James Roberts called in the National Guard because the protest had escalated when students burned down the Reserve Officers' Training Corps (ROTC) building (a facility used for training college students whose tuition is being paid for by the government in exchange for a future term in the armed services). On May 14, 1970, two students were killed by police at Jackson State University in Mississippi. Students at that all-black school were protesting both the war and racial discrimination.

The Kent State killings divided many Americans. Some were shocked that troops would fire at unarmed students. Others thought that the antiwar protests showed disrespect to the government, which they believed had a right to use violence, if necessary, to end them.

CHAPTER 7

The Fall of the South

In January 1973, President Nixon announced that the United States and North Vietnam had reached an agreement to end the war. The treaty let the North Vietnamese keep their troops in the south. The North Vietnamese would not accept peace without that provision, and because American citizens and lawmakers were demanding that the war end, Nixon agreed. That decision upset President Thieu of South Vietnam, who did not want the NVA in his country. But U.S. officials told Thieu that if he did not accept the agreement, they would cut off all aid.

Thieu knew he needed that aid if he was to have any chance of staying in power.

Under the Paris Peace Accords, as the final treaty was called, all the fighting would stop in South Vietnam. The United States agreed to pull all its remaining troops out of the country. Both sides would swap their prisoners of war. A new government with both communists and Thieu would set up elections for the south. Eventually, North and South Vietnam would discuss reuniting to form one

▼ National security adviser Henry Kissinger (right) shakes the hand of North Vietnamese delegate Le Duc Tho in Paris, France, on January 23, 1973, after reaching an agreement for restoring peace in Vietnam.

country. Under a separate accord, the United States also agreed to end its bombing in Laos.

Under the accords, the United States had sixty days to pull out its remaining troops. The last U.S. forces left South Vietnam on March 29, 1973. In private, however, Nixon promised Thieu that the United States would give up to $2 billion in aid to South Vietnam and "respond with full force should the [Paris] settlement be violated by North Vietnam." U.S. planes continued to bomb Cambodia, where communist rebels were fighting the pro-U.S. government. U.S. leaders expected the North Vietnamese to end their support for the rebels, who were called the Khmer Rouge (Red Cambodians). The Khmer Rouge, however, continued to fight on its own.

The bombing in Cambodia ended in August 1973, yet fighting still went on there. In South Vietnam, both the NVA and the ARVN broke the cease-fire they had agreed to in the Paris accords. As they battled each other, North Vietnam sneaked more communist soldiers into the south. Thieu did not believe there would be peace in his country, and he feared losing control to the communists. In addition, events in the United States made it hard for Nixon to keep all his past promises to Thieu.

By the fall of 1973, the United States was facing growing problems of its own. Prices for many goods were creeping upward, some Americans were losing their jobs, and the price of oil exploded in 1974. Congress was tired of spending money in South Vietnam and wanted to focus on domestic issues.

To prevent the country from getting involved in future long, losing battles like the Vietnam War, Congress passed a new law regarding the power of all presidents. Under the U.S. Constitution, the president is the commander in chief, who controls the

POWs and MIAs

Starting in February 1973, North Vietnam released 591 U.S. prisoners of war (POWs). It is believed that North Vietnam held back hundreds of others. Most American POWs were pilots shot down over Southeast Asia. Under international law, North Vietnam was not supposed to mistreat its prisoners, but some reported being tortured and others died in captivity. Hoping to avoid torture or death, some of the prisoners tried to escape, and a few hundred were successful. Another 2,400 U.S. troops were listed as missing in action (MIA). Their bodies were not found, and North Vietnam claimed not to know if they were alive or dead. Reports of American POWs still alive in Southeast Asia after the war have never been proven.

The *Mayaguez* Incident

In May 1975, the U.S. military had one last battle in Southeast Asia. Cambodian soldiers stopped a U.S. merchant ship, the *Mayaguez*, and took the ship's crew to a small island. President Ford then sent in military forces to rescue the Americans. The troops attacked the island and the ship, losing forty-one men during the mission. What Ford and his advisers did not know at the time was that the Cambodians were already preparing to release the prisoners. Despite the loss of life, many Americans supported Ford's actions. They were glad to see him act forcefully after the United States just lost the war in Vietnam.

Fast Fact

After the Paris Peace Accords were signed, Secretary of Defense Laird announced an end to the draft in the United States. A draft has not been used since, and the U.S. military now uses only volunteers.

military and sends troops into battle. Yet only Congress has the power to declare war. Congress had never declared war in Vietnam, though it did allow the president to send troops there under the Gulf of Tonkin Resolution of 1964. Now, in 1973, Congress passed the War Powers Act in order to "insure that the . . . judgment of both the Congress and the President will apply to the introduction of United States Armed Forces into hostilities," or situations where violence seems likely to occur. The War Powers Act gave presidents the power to use troops for only sixty days without approval from Congress. After that time, Congress had to declare war or approve keeping the troops in a hostile situation. Otherwise, the troops had to come home.

Nixon was also facing another crisis that would come to be known simply as "Watergate." The Watergate is a hotel and office building in Washington, D.C. The Democratic Party had an office there. On June 17, 1972, five men associated with Nixon's "plumbers" broke into that office and were arrested. Nixon's staff insisted that no one at the White House was involved in the Watergate break-in. But by 1973, evidence showed that Nixon and his advisers knew about the break-in and had lied about it. Congress and the courts examined his role in the scandal.

Faced with what seemed almost certain impeachment, Nixon announced on August 8, 1974, that he would resign the next day, before the Senate would meet to determine his guilt. Nixon was the first U.S. president to resign from office in the history of the United States.

The Last Months of the War

After Nixon resigned in August 1974, Vice President Gerald Ford took over as president. He led the

The Vietnam War

United States through the last months of the Vietnam War. Ford had supported the Vietnam War since the beginning. He and Henry Kissinger still hoped to give Thieu aid so the South Vietnamese could continue the battle against the communists. Congress, however, had reduced the level of financial aid sent to South Vietnam. As Kissinger later said, "The South Vietnamese army was not only required to fight alone, but it had to cut their ammunition [spending] by 70 percent, air power by 80 percent."

At the same time, North Vietnam was increasing its attacks in the south. Its forces were slowly closing in on Saigon. By April 1975, the NVA was just outside the South Vietnamese capital. The few Americans still in the city prepared to leave, and the U.S. government tried to help South Vietnamese leaders flee as well. They faced jail or even death once the communists took control. On the morning of April 30, a U.S. Navy captain in Saigon noted that "instances of hostile fire increased markedly." Finally, before the end of the day, the last Americans left Vietnam and the North Vietnamese controlled the country.

With the fall of Saigon, the communists had achieved Ho Chi Minh's goal of long ago—creating a united Vietnam under communist rule. Communists now also ruled in Cambodia and would soon take power in Laos. For the first time ever, the United States had lost a war, and it had failed to stop the spread of communism in Southeast Asia.

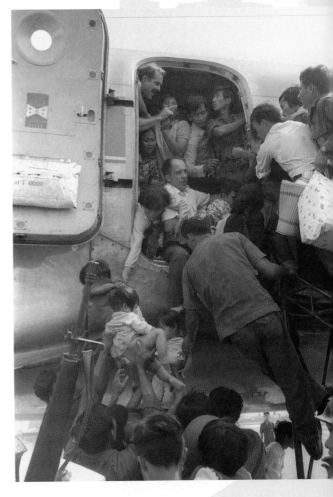

▼ Panicking South Vietnamese civilians scramble to board a U.S. aircraft evacuating the town of Nha Trang, on the coast of Vietnam, on April 1, 1975. As communist forces advanced on the nearby town of Qui Nhon, hundreds of villagers were airlifted to Saigon.

CHAPTER 8

After the War

The end of U.S. military action in Southeast Asia did not end the killing there. In Cambodia, the Khmer Rouge seized power. Their leader was Pol Pot. He killed several million Cambodians who opposed his plan to create a communist society. Within several years, Vietnam tried to assert control over the Cambodian communists by launching an invasion to wipe out the Khmer Rouge, leading to war between the two countries. In 1979, China attacked Vietnam, in retaliation for Vietnam's attack on Cambodia, as well as because of long-standing tensions between China and Vietnam.

The Refugees

The Vietnam War and the fighting after it caused hundreds of thousands of Southeast Asians to flee the violence in their homelands for safety in other parts of Asia and the United States. Many of these **refugees** risked their lives sailing on rickety boats and rafts. Most of these so-called "boat people" ended up in special camps, mostly in Thailand, where they waited to find out where they could resettle.

In 1975, Congress passed the first of several laws that allowed large

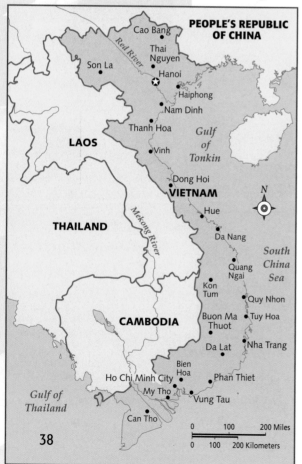

▼ Vietnam today, shown in pink. South Vietnam and North Vietnam were unified in 1975 when northern communist forces defeated the South Vietnamese. The city of Saigon is now called Ho Chi Minh City.

PEOPLE'S REPUBLIC OF CHINA

Cao Bang
Red River
Thai Nguyen
Son La
Hanoi
Haiphong
Nam Dinh
Thanh Hoa
LAOS
Vinh
Gulf of Tonkin
Dong Hoi
VIETNAM
N
Hue
THAILAND
Mekong River
Da Nang
South China Sea
Quang Ngai
Kon Tum
Quy Nhon
Buon Ma Thuot
Tuy Hoa
CAMBODIA
Da Lat
Nha Trang
Bien Hoa
Ho Chi Minh City
Phan Thiet
My Tho
Vung Tau
Gulf of Thailand
Can Tho

0   100   200 Miles
0   100   200 Kilometers

numbers of Southeast Asian refugees to come to the United States. Before this, few immigrants had come from Vietnam, Cambodia, or Laos. Many of the new arrivals went to California, which already had a large Asian population. By 1990, more than 500,000 Southeast Asians had settled across the United States, and the total reached more than one million later that decade. One group of new arrivals was the Hmong, a tribal people from Laos, who had helped the U.S. government battle communists in their homeland. The Hmong refugees settled on the West Coast and in the upper Midwest—Minnesota and Wisconsin. Some Hmong were still arriving in the twenty-first century, after spending years at refugee camps in Thailand. Other refugees were the children of Vietnamese women and U.S. soldiers. In 1987, Congress passed a law to make it easier for them to move to the United States. About twenty-five thousand of these Amerasians soon entered the country.

The newcomers sometimes struggled to find homes and jobs. Most did not speak English, and they often faced discrimination. The Southeast Asians were mostly Buddhist, not Christian, and they reminded some people of the U.S. failure in the Vietnam War. Over time, however, the refugees and their children learned English and adjusted to American culture. Today, the children of the original refugees are finding success in many fields, just as the children of earlier immigrants have done. One Hmong immigrant said in 2004, "Compared to other refugee and immigrant groups, the Hmong have come so far in a shorter amount of time."

The Veterans

The Vietnam War had a lasting effect on the Americans who fought in it. Many returning veterans felt the effects of the war long after they came home. Thousands were disabled because of wounds suffered during the war. At times, they struggled to find jobs or adjust to their new life with disabilities. Others wrestled with post-traumatic stress disorder, a mental disability caused by the experiences of combat, especially killing others and seeing friends die. Post-traumatic stress disorder causes many problems such as depression, anxiety, and health issues related to stress, such as heart disease. Some veterans had become addicted to alcohol or drugs while in Vietnam. One government study said that as many as 30 percent of the U.S. soldiers who went to Vietnam tried heroin, and even more smoked marijuana.

Many returned veterans also struggled with the toxic effects of the defoliant Agent Orange, which had been used to strip leaves from trees and deprive Vietcong soldiers of cover in the jungle. Agent Orange contains a harmful chemical called dioxin. Exposure to dioxin can result in a variety of cancers, skin diseases, and birth defects in people exposed to it, their children, and even their grandchildren. As many as one million Vietnamese babies have been born with physical defects because their parents were exposed to dioxin. Some U.S. veterans also say they have health problems related to their handling of Agent Orange during the war. The group Vietnam Veterans of America is still asking the U.S. government to aid veterans affected by dioxin.

The veterans' readjustment to life as civilians was made more difficult by the antiwar attitude of many Americans. After most past wars, soldiers had been

▼ In this 1966 photograph, U.S. Air Force planes spray the chemical defoliant Agent Orange over dense forests in South Vietnam in order to kill plant life and expose Vietcong troops hiding in the jungle.

treated as heroes. Many Vietnam veterans, however, were badly treated on their return. The lack of support for the war and the report of atrocities led some antiwar protesters to taunt the soldiers.

Starting in about 1980, Vietnam veterans began calling for the country to officially honor their service and the service of the thousands killed during the war. In 1982, the U.S. government opened the Vietnam Veterans Memorial in Washington, D.C. On a large wall of black granite in the shape of a V is carved the name of every American military person who died in Vietnam. The memorial also features separate statues of soldiers on patrol and army nurses taking care of a wounded soldier. With the memorial, many veterans finally felt they had won the respect they had not received for their efforts during the war.

For years after the war, Vietnam and the United States did not have diplomatic relations and the U.S. government prevented U.S. companies from doing business with the Vietnamese. In the early 1990s, however, President George H. W. Bush began letting some American groups travel to Vietnam, and in 1995, President Bill Clinton opened official diplomatic relations with the country. U.S. veterans had their first chance to go back to Vietnam to see where they had fought and where their friends had died and to meet some of the Vietnamese they had once fought against. U.S. veteran Michael Austin wrote about one former Vietnamese soldier, "Technically a Communist and my former enemy, Tru was also one of the most decent and understanding men I could hope to meet."

A Change of Thinking

The end of the Vietnam War did not end the Cold War between the United States and the Soviet Union. The Vietnam War did, however, make the United

Senators McCain and Kerry: Different Parties

Senator John McCain, a Republican from Arizona, spent more than five years as a POW during the Vietnam War. Senator John Kerry, a Democrat from Massachusetts, received three medals for his service in Vietnam. When he returned home, he became a leader of Vietnam Veterans Against the War. The two veterans disagree on many issues, including whether or not the United States should have fought in Vietnam. But in 1992, they worked together to try to learn if Vietnam still held U.S. soldiers listed as MIA. The answer, they said, was no. Their work led the way to President Clinton's opening relations with Vietnam. In 2004, Kerry became the first Vietnam veteran to run for president, but he was defeated by George W. Bush.

Fast Fact

New names continue to be added to the wall of the Vietnam Veterans Memorial as the government learns about men and women who died in Vietnam or from wounds they suffered there. Four names were added in 2005.

States less eager to send troops to fight in a foreign country. Military and political leaders were willing to go to war only if they believed the United States could win quickly or faced a direct threat to its safety. That attitude continues to be held by military and political leaders as well as many U.S. citizens.

In the years since the Vietnam War, scholars, soldiers, and politicians have debated why the United States lost in Vietnam. Some say that President Johnson should not have tried to fight a limited war but should have sent in more troops and extended the fighting to North Vietnam. Others say that the United States should have continued to support South Vietnam after 1973, as President Nixon had promised, and that such aid would have prevented North Vietnam from taking over the country. As one North Vietnamese leader later wrote, South Vietnam's President Thieu was forced to fight "a poor man's war." He could not win without U.S. help.

On the other side, some scholars argue that the United States made a mistake by seeing Vietnam as strictly a Cold War battle. Ho Chi Minh did want to spread communism in Southeast Asia, but he wanted to be independent of both the Soviet Union and China. If free elections had been held in 1956, he probably would have won, because many Vietnamese respected him for his struggle to win independence from both Japan and France. Most of South Vietnam's leaders, meanwhile, did not have much popular support. It is estimated that the United States spent about $150 billion and lost more than fifty-eight thousand people in its effort to prop up a weak government.

▼ Vietnam today is influenced by the United States, its top trading partner, as seen in this photograph of people wheeling a Coca-Cola vending machine past the opera house in Hanoi in July 2005. The year 2005 marked the tenth anniversary of diplomatic ties between the two nations.

The Vietnam War

As early as 1949, some military leaders did not think the United States should get involved in Vietnam. Doing so, one member of the Joint Chiefs of Staff said, would "likely in the long run...create more problems than it solves and cause more damage than benefit." President Harry Truman and four presidents after him chose to ignore that advice. Robert McNamara, the former secretary of defense, wrote in 1995, "We...acted according to what we thought were the principles and traditions of this nation.... Yet we were wrong, terribly wrong."

The U.S. experience in Vietnam still shapes debate over other military actions. In 2003, the United States invaded Iraq. The U.S. military quickly forced Iraqi leader Saddam Hussein from power and took control of the country. Soon, however, U.S. troops were fighting Iraqi insurgents and foreigners who opposed the U.S. presence. The insurgents used guerrilla tactics, as the Vietcong had, such as staging sudden ambushes and blending in with civilians.

Some critics say that President George W. Bush has done what presidents before him had tried to avoid: He has created "another Vietnam" by failing to send enough troops to Iraq at the start of the war and failing to foresee strong resistance by the Iraqi people. Most experts say that the two wars are different in many ways. Yet, in 2006, after three years of fighting, U.S. troops are still being killed, and some Americans think that the president and his advisers—like Kennedy and Johnson—did not tell the truth about why the United States had started the war.

The Vietnam War cost more money than any U.S. war before it. It was also the country's longest war, and it divided the nation more than any other conflict except the Civil War. The issues raised by the Vietnam War will continue to be discussed for decades to come.

In the Open

After the Cold War ended, many communist nations became democratic. Their new governments released documents about the Cold War era that had been kept secret before. Even countries that remain communist, such as China and Vietnam, released old records about the Vietnam War. These records have given U.S. historians important new knowledge about the communists' actions and goals during the war. For example, Soviet leaders thought for many years that North Vietnam could not win the war. Other records show that in 1954, Ho Chi Minh was willing to use peaceful means to try to reunite Vietnam. The release of new information will continue to shape views on the Vietnam War.

TIME LINE

1945	Vietnam declares its independence from France.
1950	President Harry Truman sends aid to France in its war to keep control of Vietnam.
1954	The Vietnamese defeat the French at Dien Bien Phu, winning their independence; Vietnam is split in two along the seventeenth parallel.
1955	With U.S. backing, Ngo Dinh Diem takes control in South Vietnam, while Ho Chi Minh is the leader in the north.
1959	North Vietnam begins direct aid to communists in South Vietnam.
1961	President John F. Kennedy begins increasing U.S. aid to South Vietnam.
1963	Diem is assassinated; Kennedy is assassinated and replaced by Lyndon Johnson.
1964	Gulf of Tonkin incident; Johnson wins approval from Congress to increase U.S. military action in Vietnam; the United States secretly carries out military actions in Laos.
1965	Major bombing of North Vietnam begins; first U.S. ground troops arrive in South Vietnam; U.S. troops battle the North Vietnamese at Ia Drang.
1967	Major peace demonstrations occur across the United States; Nguyen Van Thieu becomes president of South Vietnam.
1968	North Vietnam launches the Tet Offensive; U.S. forces recapture the city of Hue; Richard Nixon is elected U.S. president; My Lai massacre occurs.
1969	U.S. troop level reaches its peak of about 543,400; Nixon begins Vietnamization policy; U.S. bombing of Cambodia begins; Ho Chi Minh dies; largest antiwar protests to date occur across the United States.
1970	Nixon sends ground troops into Cambodia; four students are shot during an antiwar protest at Kent State University.
1971	The *Pentagon Papers* are published.
1972	Nixon visits China and the Soviet Union; Nixon's aides order a break-in at the Watergate office complex; Henry Kissinger and North Vietnam hold secret peace talks; Nixon orders massive bombing of North Vietnam.
1973	U.S. troops leave South Vietnam after the signing of the Paris Peace Accords; South and North Vietnamese continue to battle for control in the south.
1974	Congress cuts aid to South Vietnam; Nixon resigns as a result of his role in the Watergate scandal; Gerald Ford replaces Nixon as U.S. president.
1975	North Vietnam wins the Vietnam War; communist governments also come to power in Cambodia and Laos; refugees begin leaving Southeast Asia.
1982	The Vietnam Veterans Memorial opens in Washington, D.C.
1995	The United States and Vietnam establish official diplomatic relations.

GLOSSARY

accords agreements between nations or opposing groups

allies friends and supporters of a person or country

artillery large, mobile guns

atrocities horrible acts of violence, often committed by soldiers against civilians

Buddhists believers in Buddhism, a religion, founded in India and practiced largely in Asia, that follows the teaching of Buddha

cabinet the top advisers of a president or other political leader

cadres small groups of people who recruit and train others for a specific cause

candidate person seeking election to a public office

capitalism an economic system based on private property and individual rights

casualties soldiers, killed, wounded, missing, or taken prisoner during a battle

civilians citizens not in the military

civil rights legal protections for citizens

Cold War a struggle between communist and noncommunist nations, primarily the United States and the Soviet Union, to spread their competing political and economic systems around the world

commandos soldiers specially trained to operate in a small group, usually within enemy territory

communism a political system featuring one party that holds complete power and promotes government ownership of businesses and property

corrupt dishonest

covert hidden or secret

democratic relating to a government ruled by the citizens of a state, either by directly voting on issues or by electing leaders to represent their interests

diplomat government representative who discusses events and relations with foreign countries

discrimination unfair treatment of others because of their race, religion, or beliefs

domestic relating to events and policies within a country

embassy the residence and office of a country's diplomats in a foreign country

escalated increased to a large degree

guerrillas small bands of unofficial soldiers operating in occupied territory, harassing and undermining their enemy, usually by surprise attack

intelligence information gathered through spying

latitude distance north or south of Earth's equator

nationalists people who believe that their nation will benefit from being independent, rather than under foreign domination

offensive a military attack to gain ground

refugees people forced to flee their homes because of war or a natural disaster

FOR FURTHER INFORMATION

Books

Burgan, Michael. *Witness to History: The Vietnam War*. Chicago: Heinemann Library, 2005.

Caputo, Philip. *Ten Thousand Days of Thunder: A History of the Vietnam War*. New York: Atheneum Books for Young Readers, 2005.

Harrison, Paul. *The Cold War*. San Diego: Lucent Books, 2005.

Márquez, Herón. *Richard Nixon*. Minneapolis: Lerner Publications, 2003.

Schynert, Mark. *Women of the Vietnam War*. Detroit: Lucent Books, 2005.

Seah, Audrey. *Vietnam*. New York: Benchmark Books/Marshall Cavendish, 2004.

Thomas, William. *The Home Front in the Vietnam War*. Milwaukee: World Almanac Library, 2005.

William, Jean Kinney. *Lyndon B. Johnson: America's 36th President*. New York: Children's Press, 2005.

Web Sites

American Experience—Vietnam Online *www.pbs.org/wgbh/amex/vietnam/*

Lyndon B. Johnson Presidential Library—Johnson's Vietnam Anguish *www.hpol.org/lbj/vietnam/*

The Sixties Project *www3.iath.virginia.edu/sixties/*

Vietnam Veterans Memorial Fund *www.thevirtualwall.org/*

The Vietnam War *www.vietnamwar.com/*

The Wars for Vietnam *vietnam.vassar.edu/*

Publisher's note to educators and parents: Our editors have carefully reviewed these Web sites to ensure that they are suitable for children. Many Web sites change frequently, however, and we cannot guarantee that a site's future contents will continue to meet our high standards of quality and educational value. Be advised that children should be closely supervised whenever they access the Internet.

INDEX

About the Author

As an editor at *Weekly Reader* for six years, Michael Burgan created educational material for an interactive online service and wrote on current events. Now a freelance author, Michael has written more than ninety books for children and young adults, including books on science, historical events, and great Americans. Michael has a B.A. in history from the University of Connecticut. He resides in Chicago.